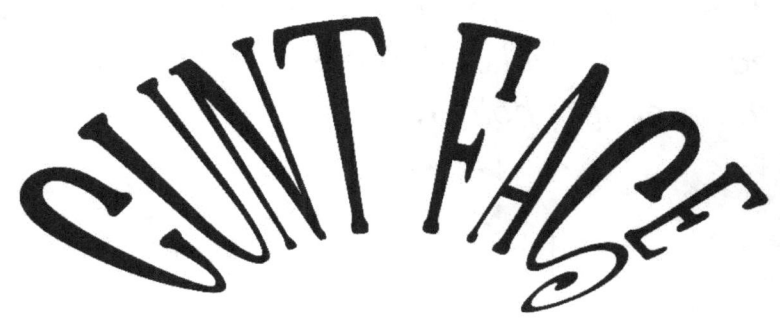

SWEAR WORD COLORING BOOK

The Universe Adult Coloring Book
featured with beautiful geometry

By

Florence Clark

Happy Coloring!

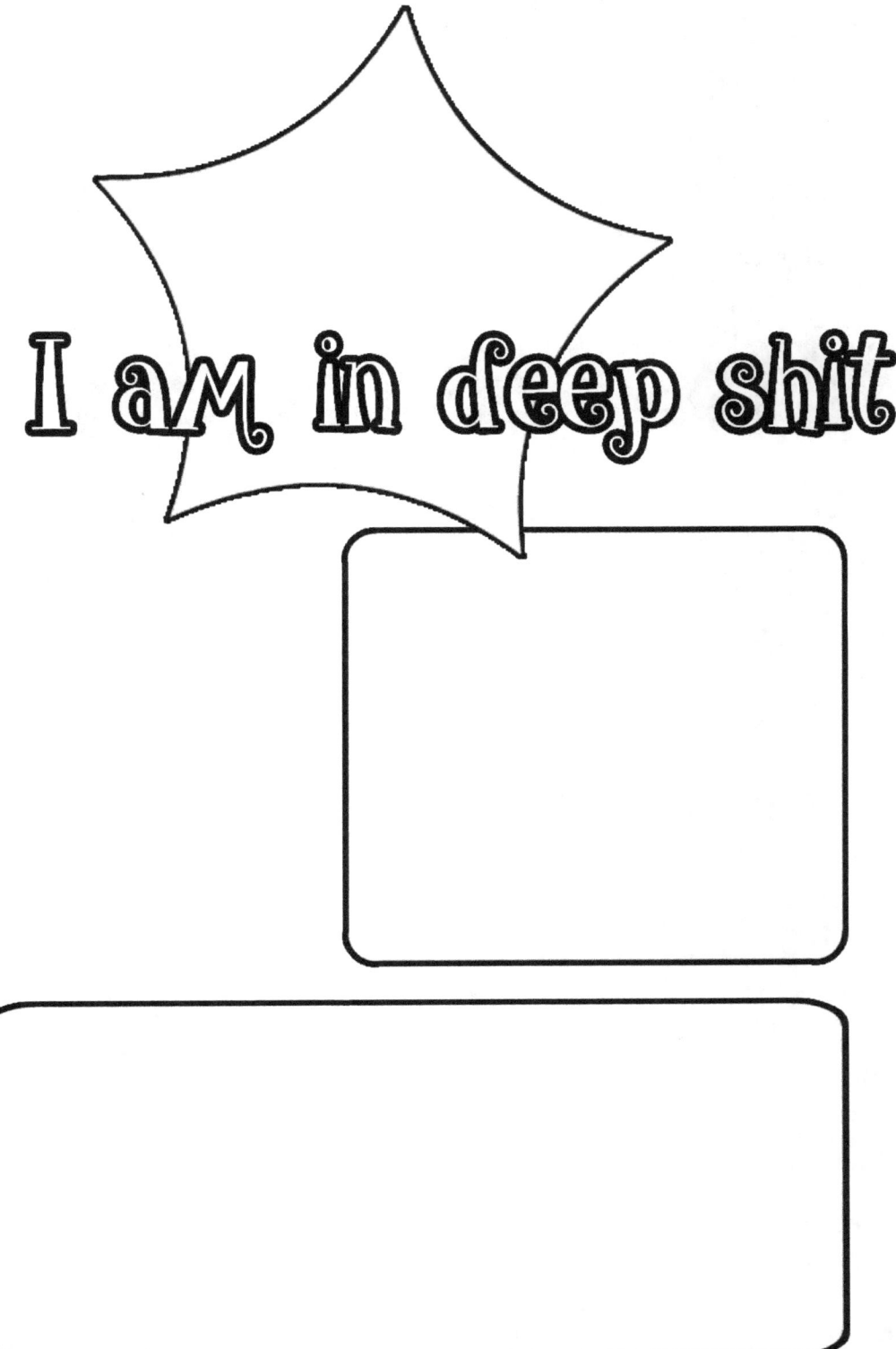

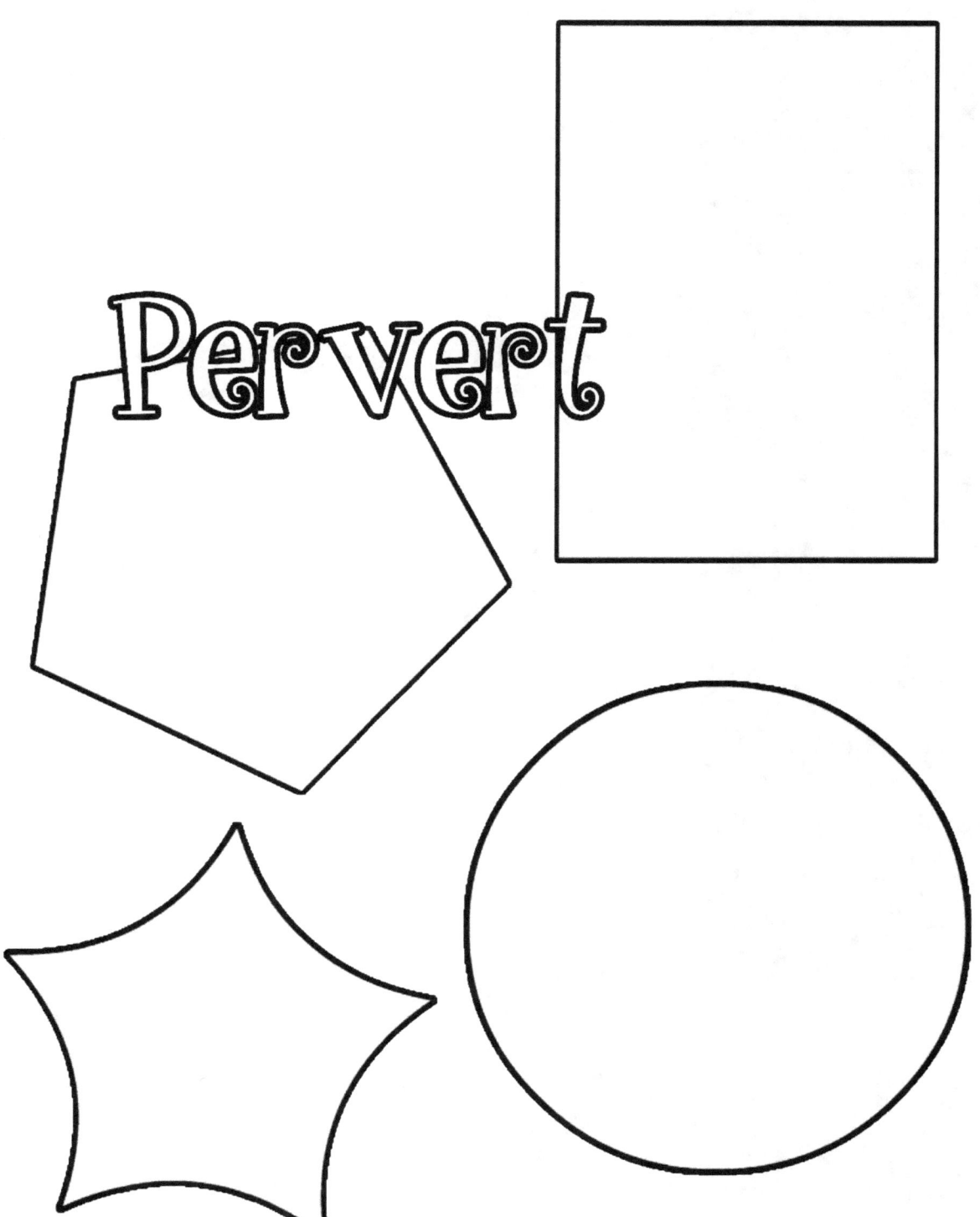

Go jerk yourself

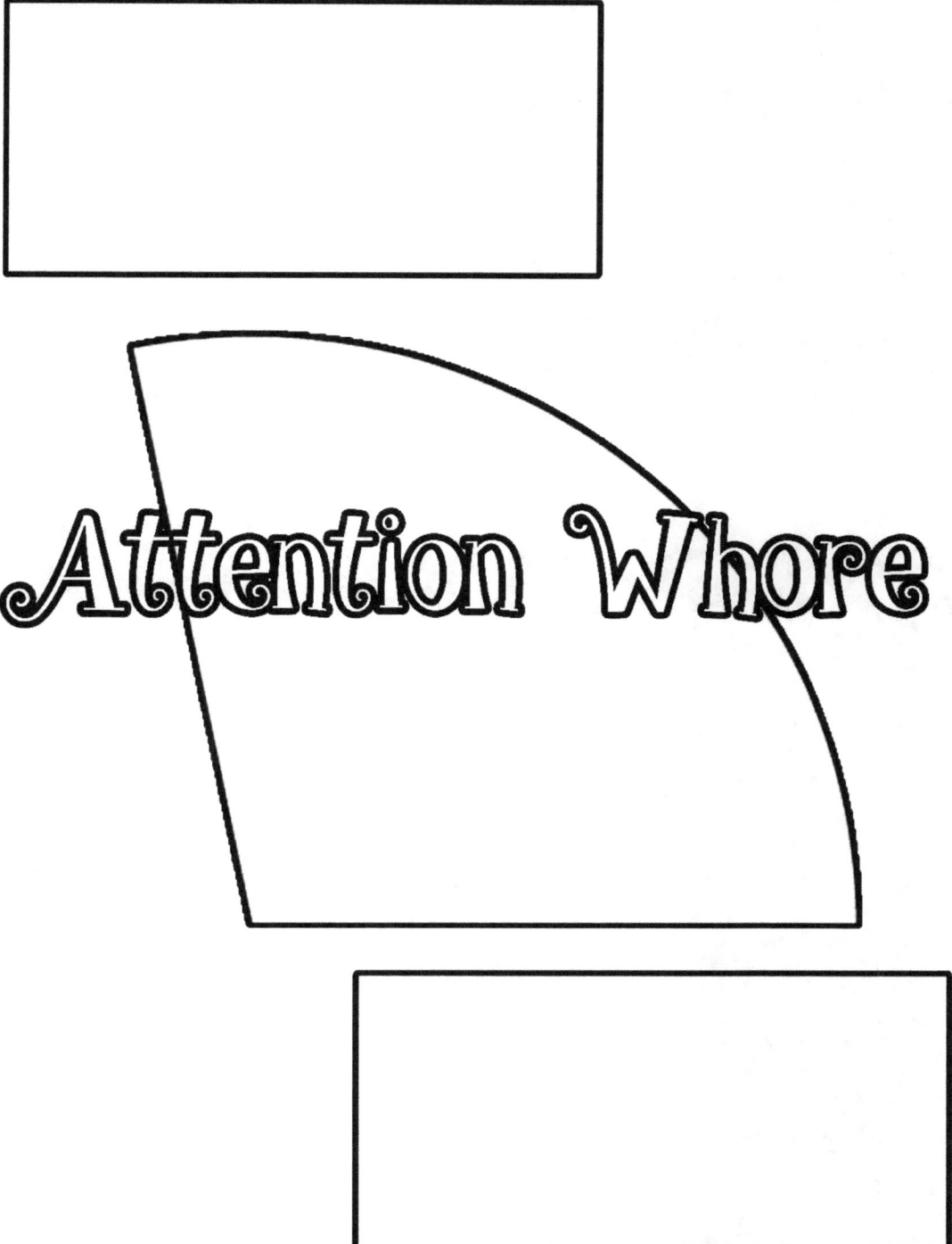

Attention Whore

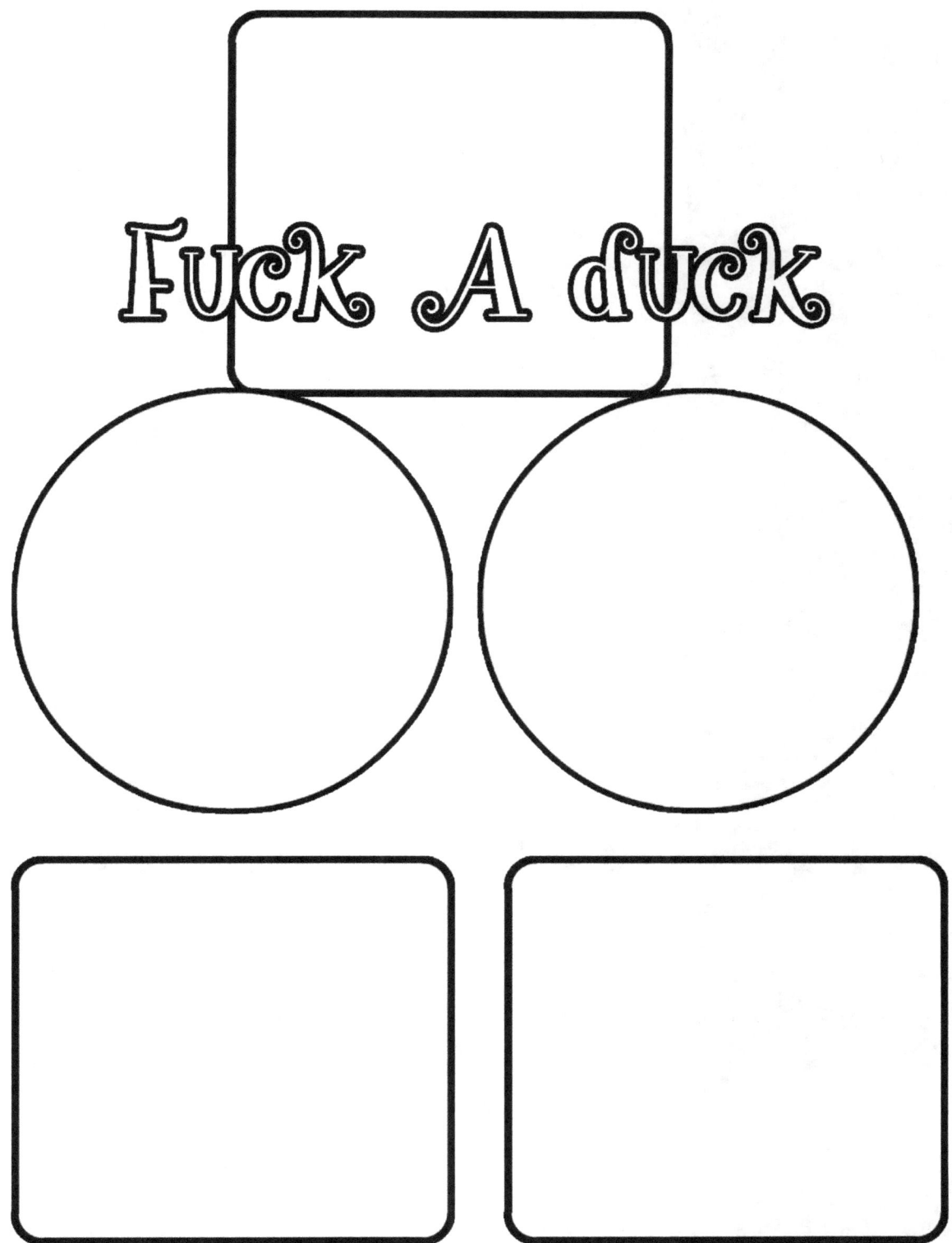

Fuck A duck

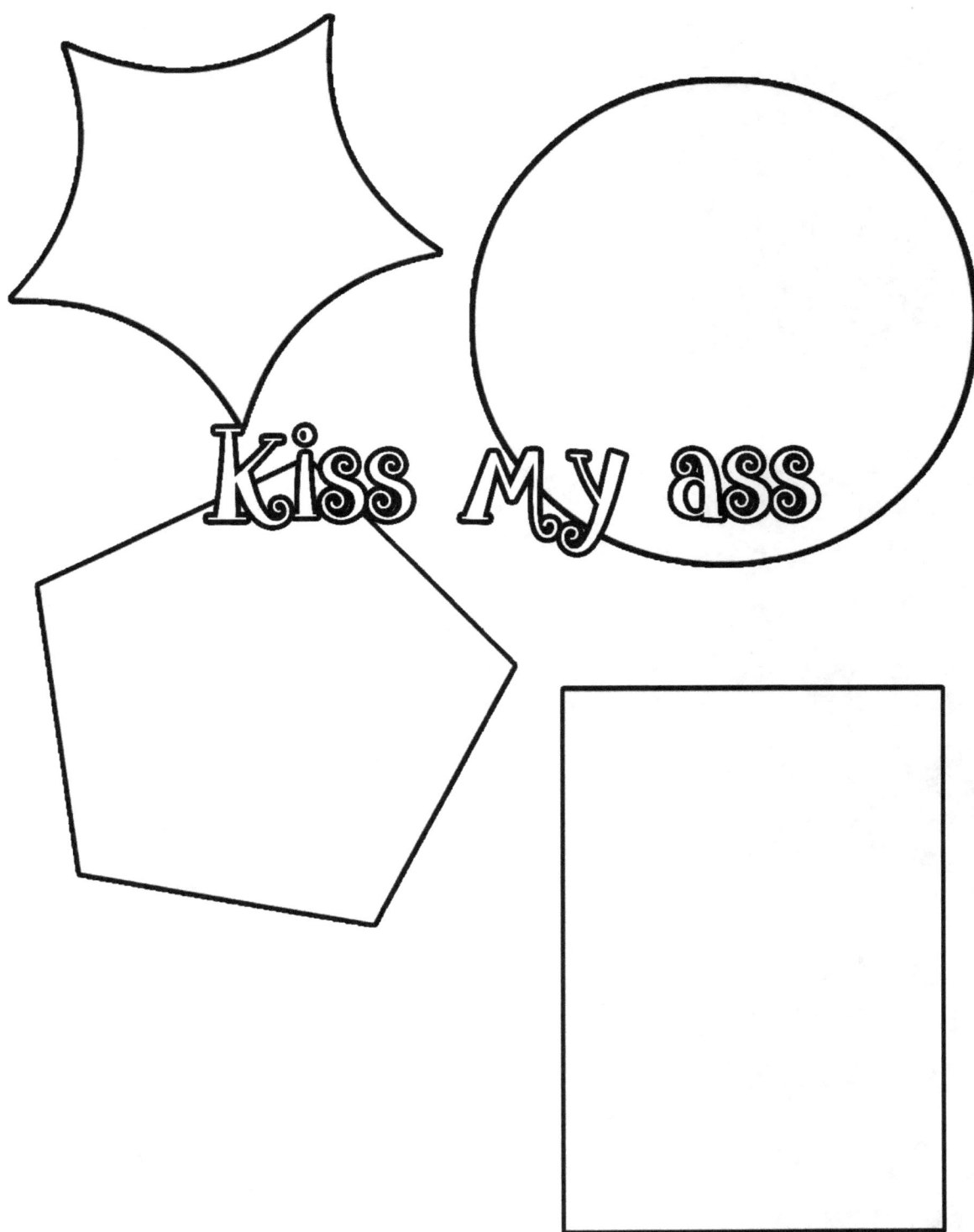

Kiss my ass

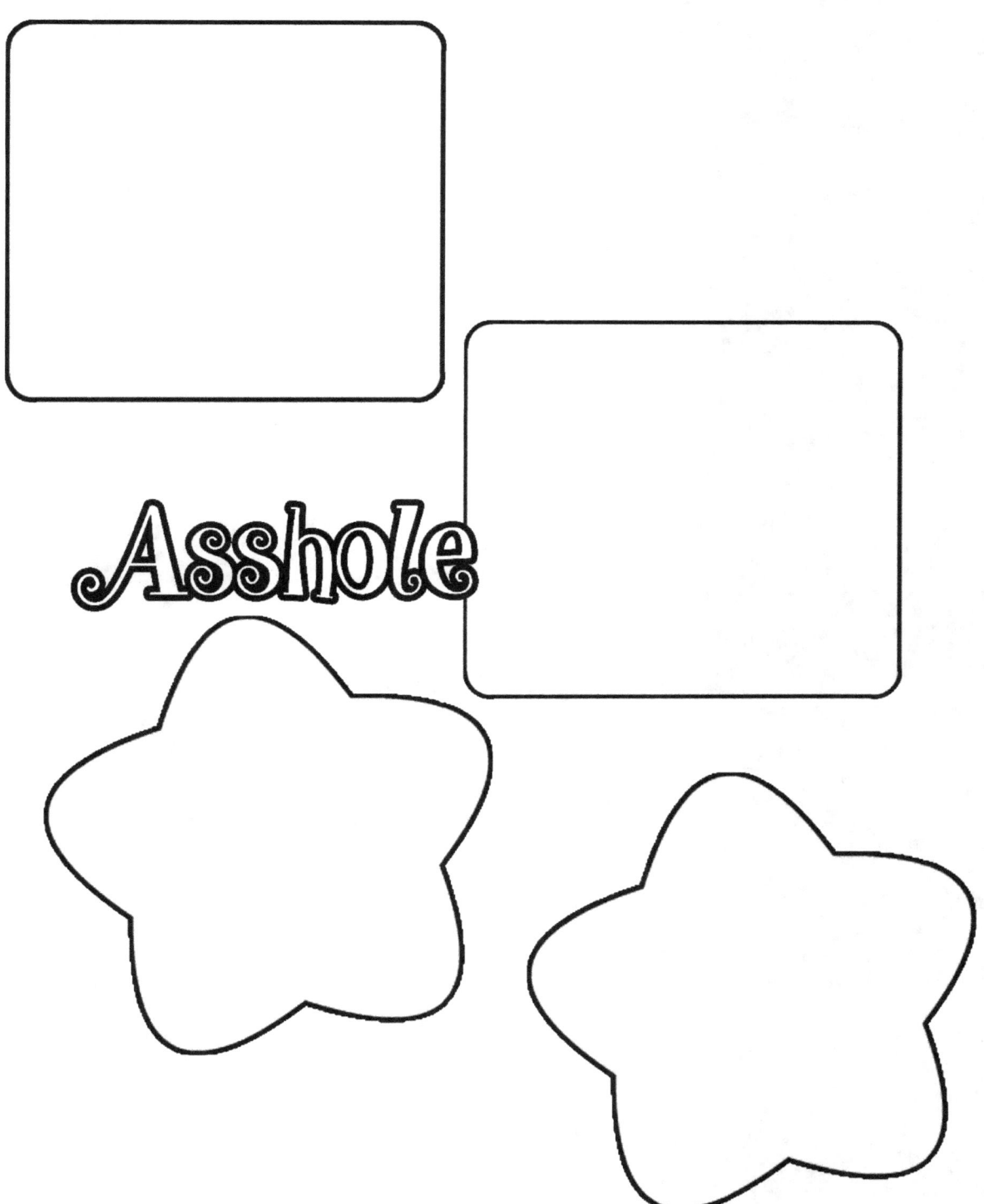

Asshole

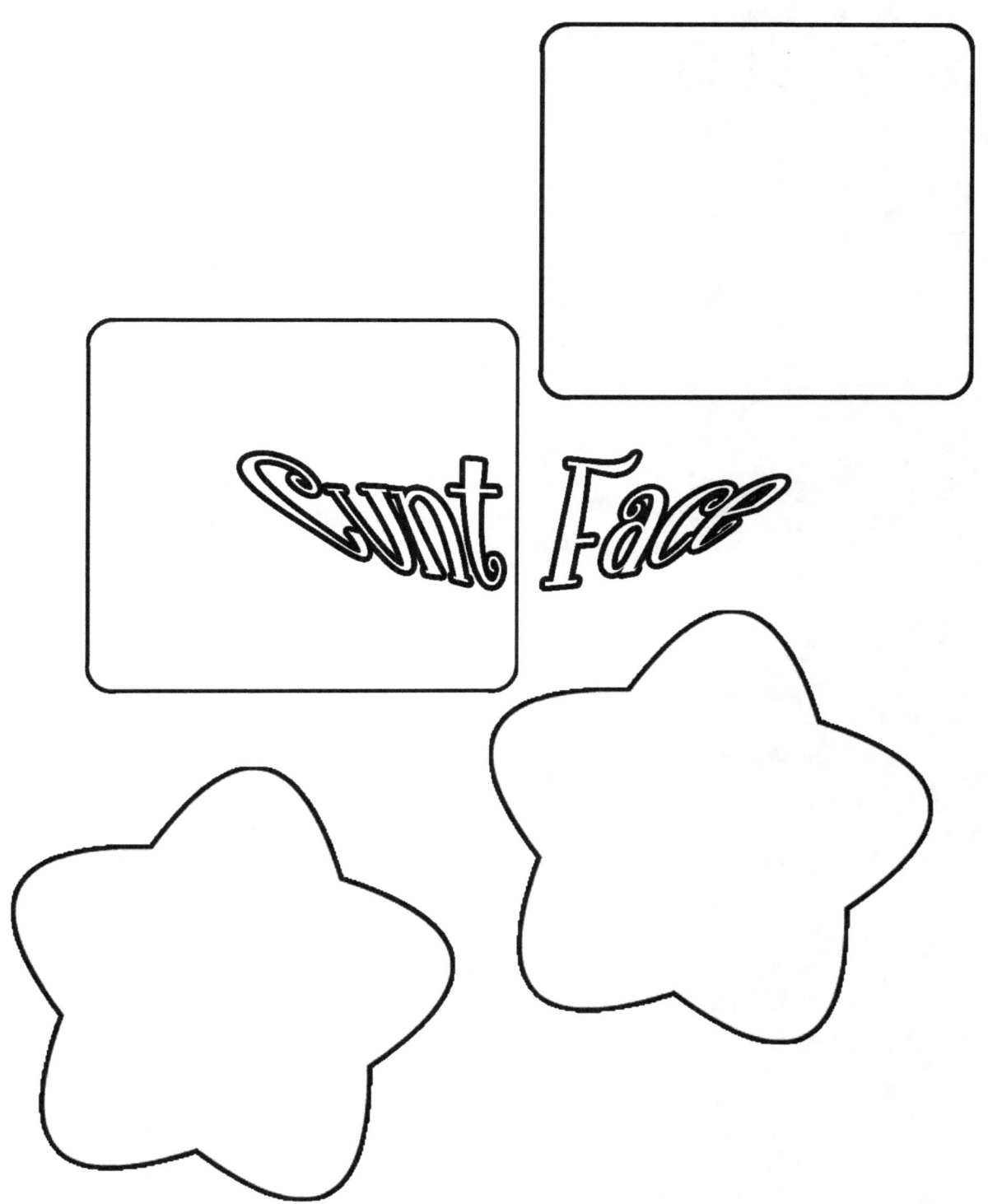

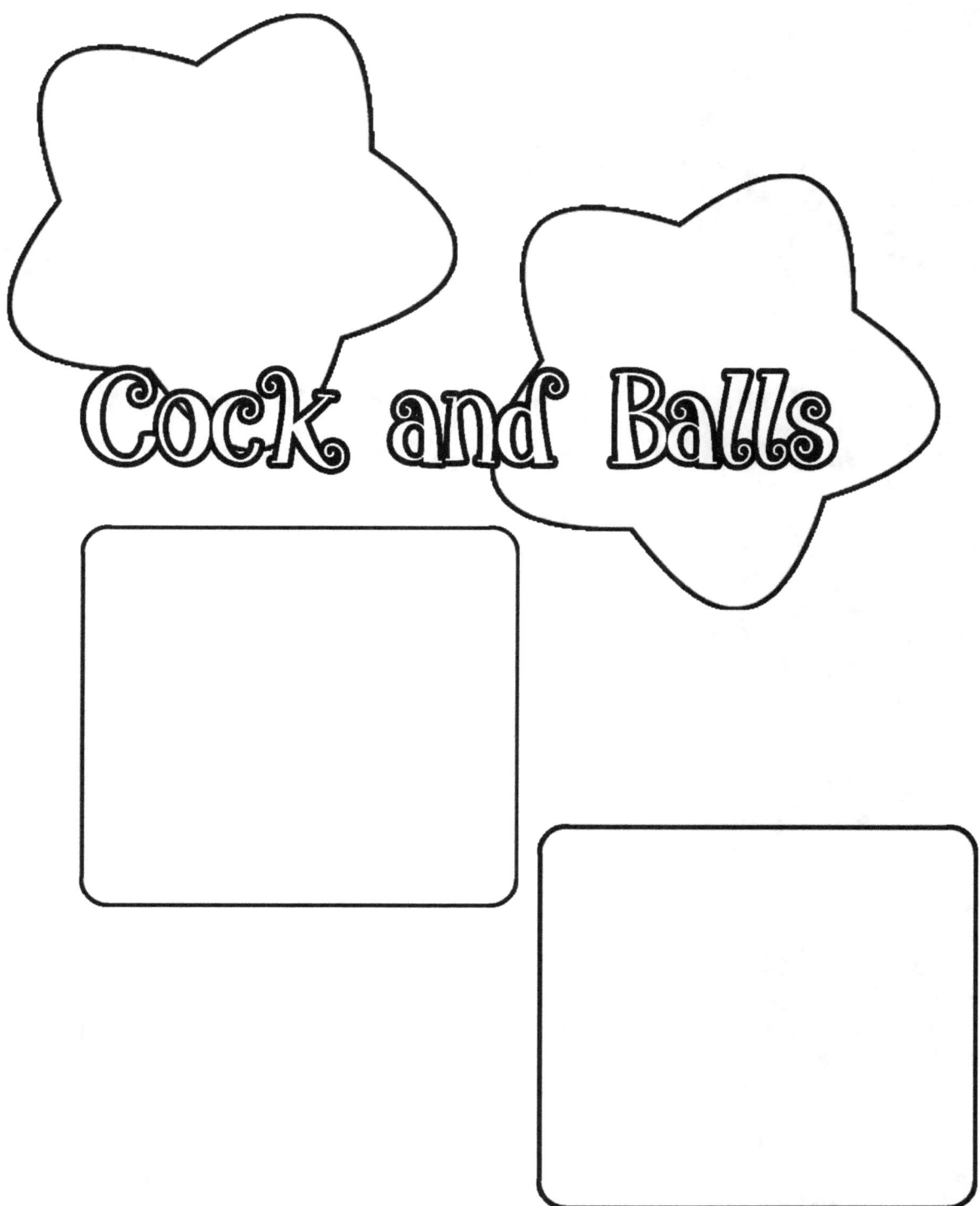

Cock and Balls

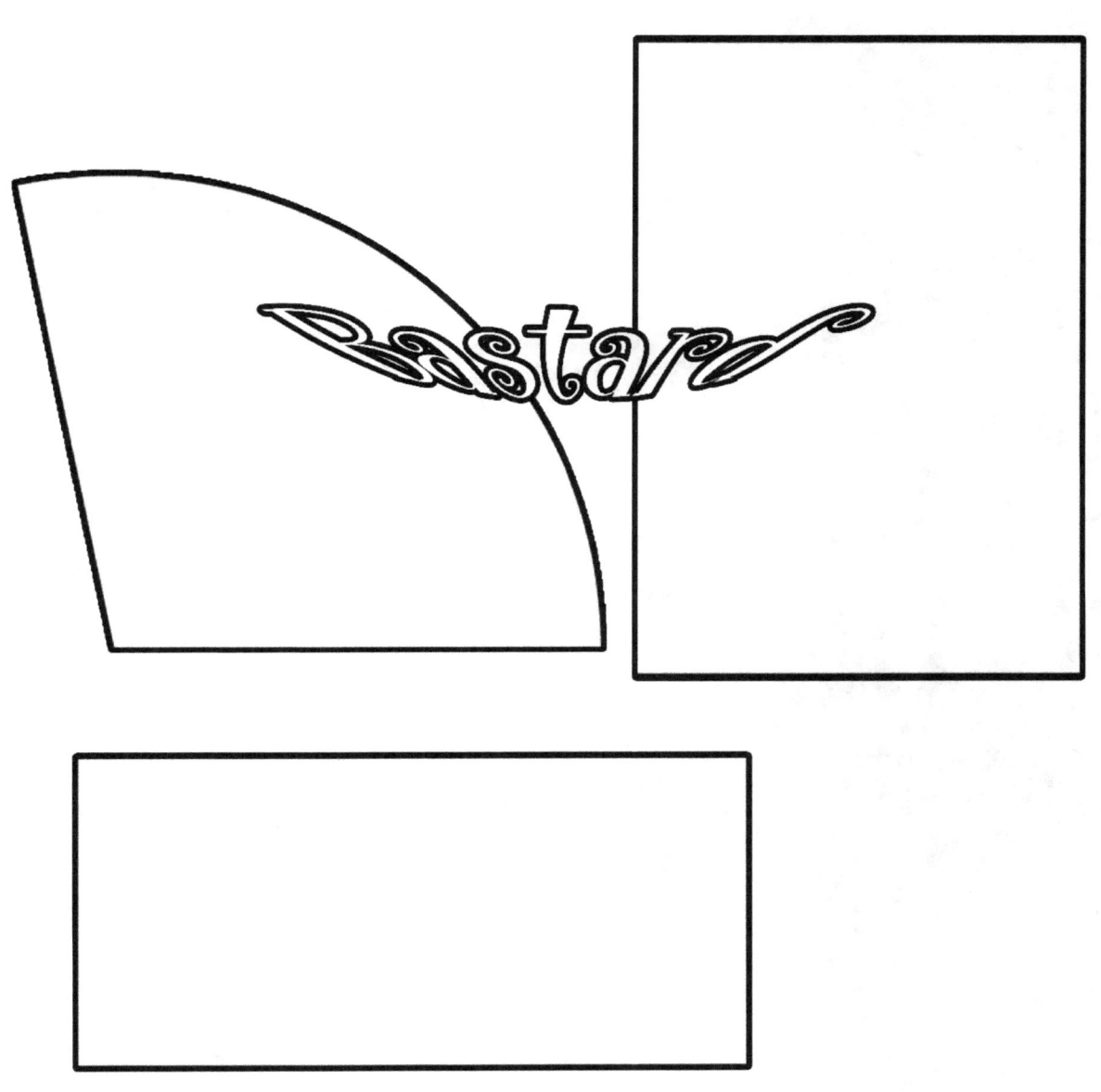

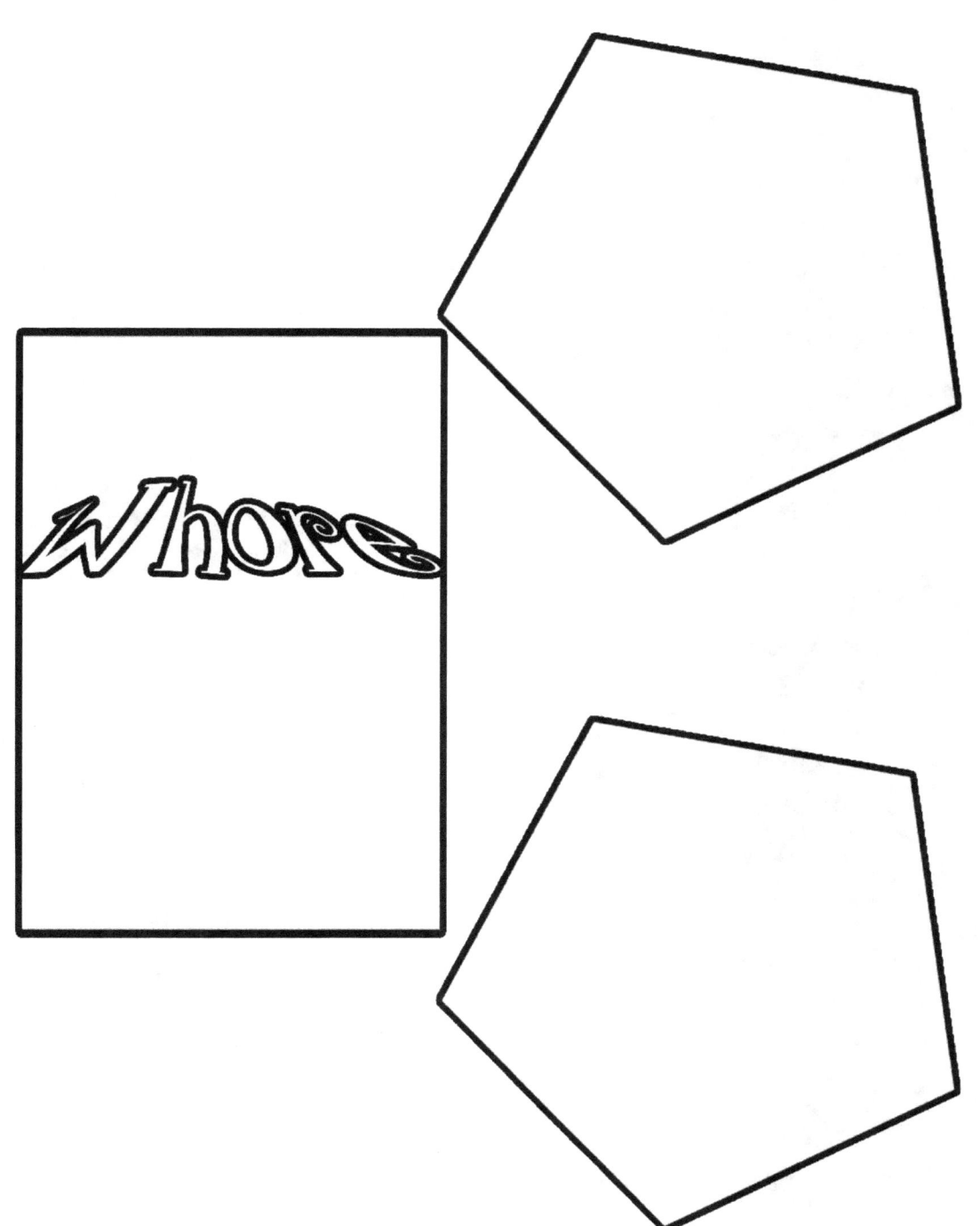

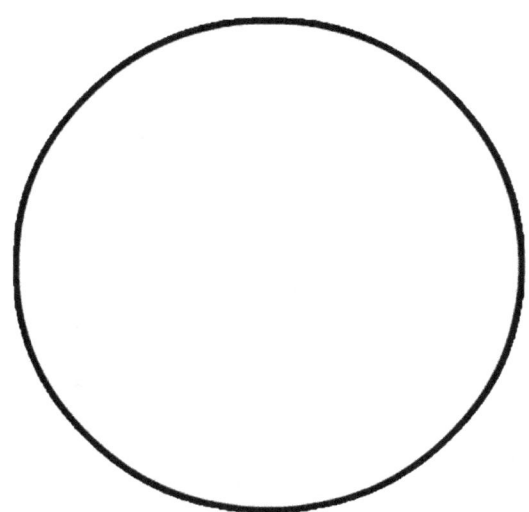

Batshit crazy

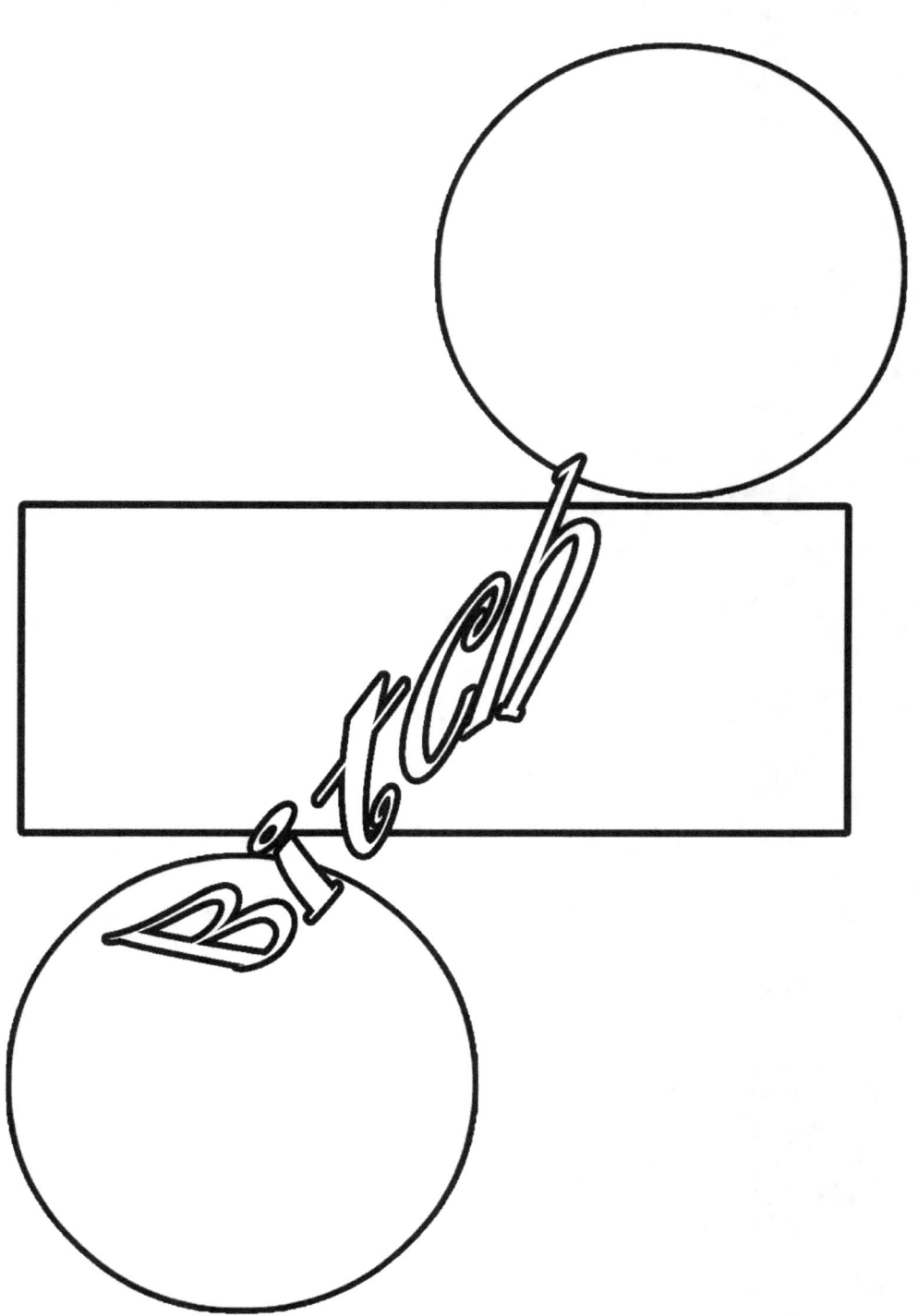

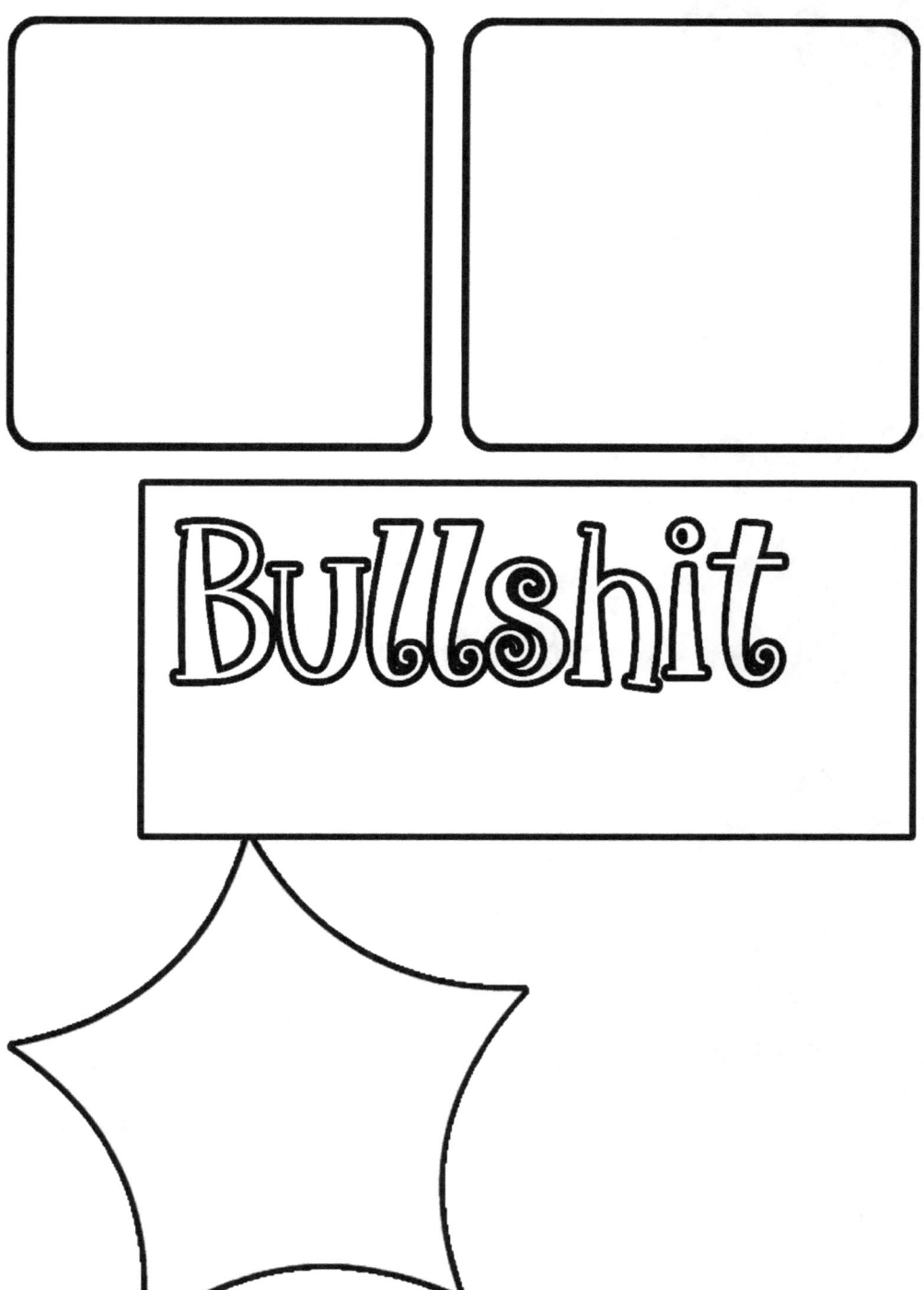

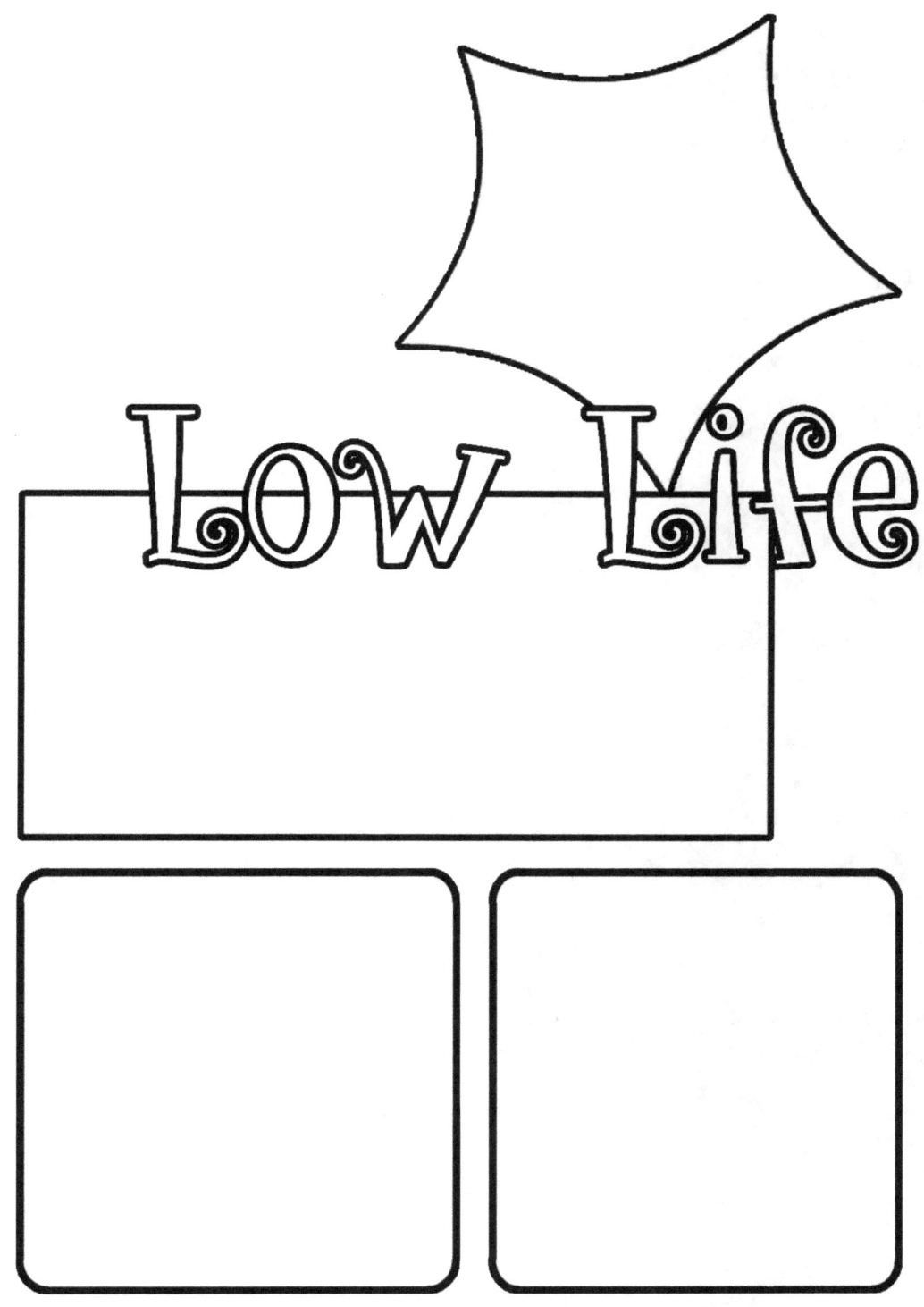

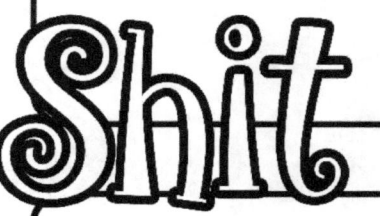

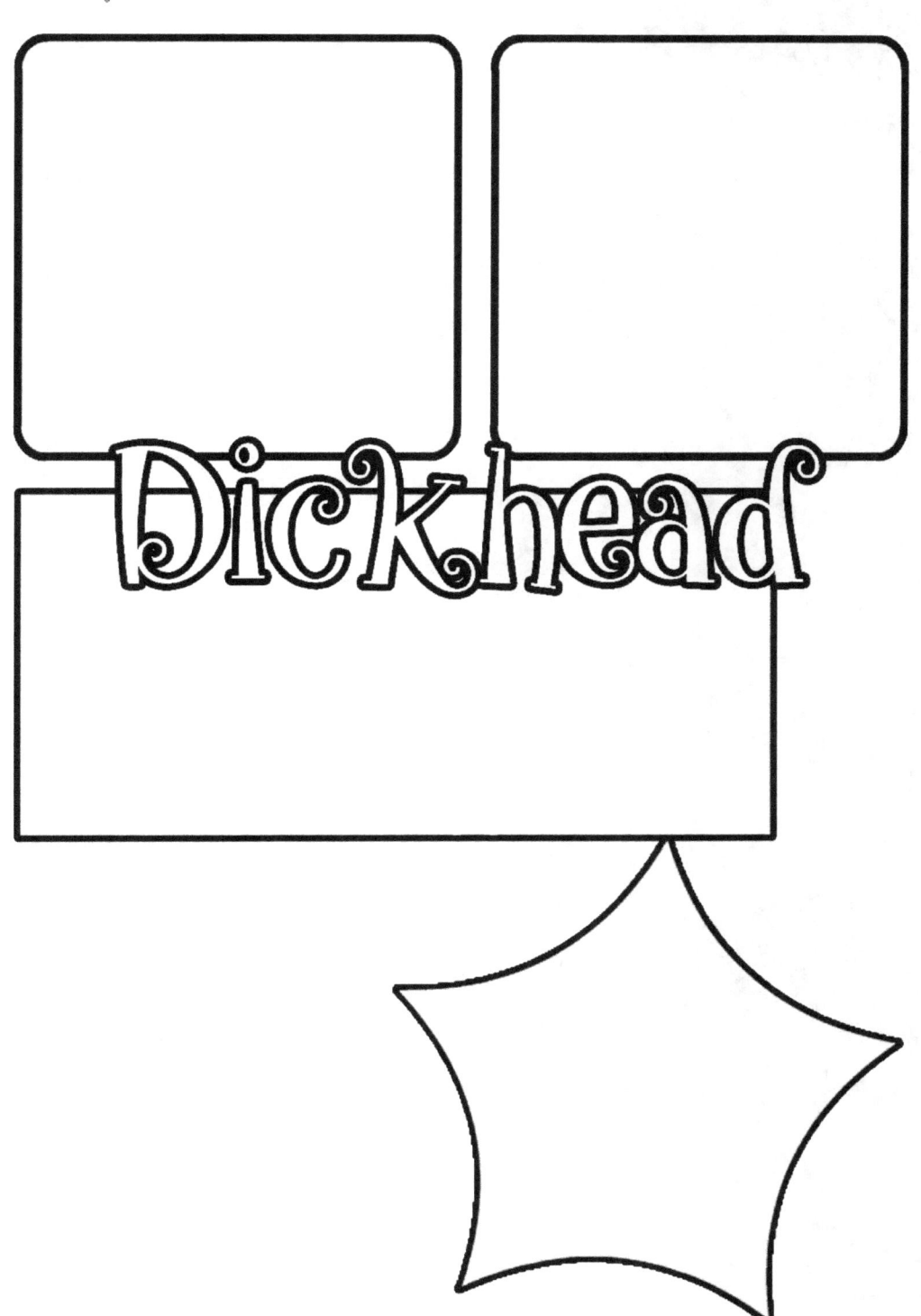

Zero fucks given

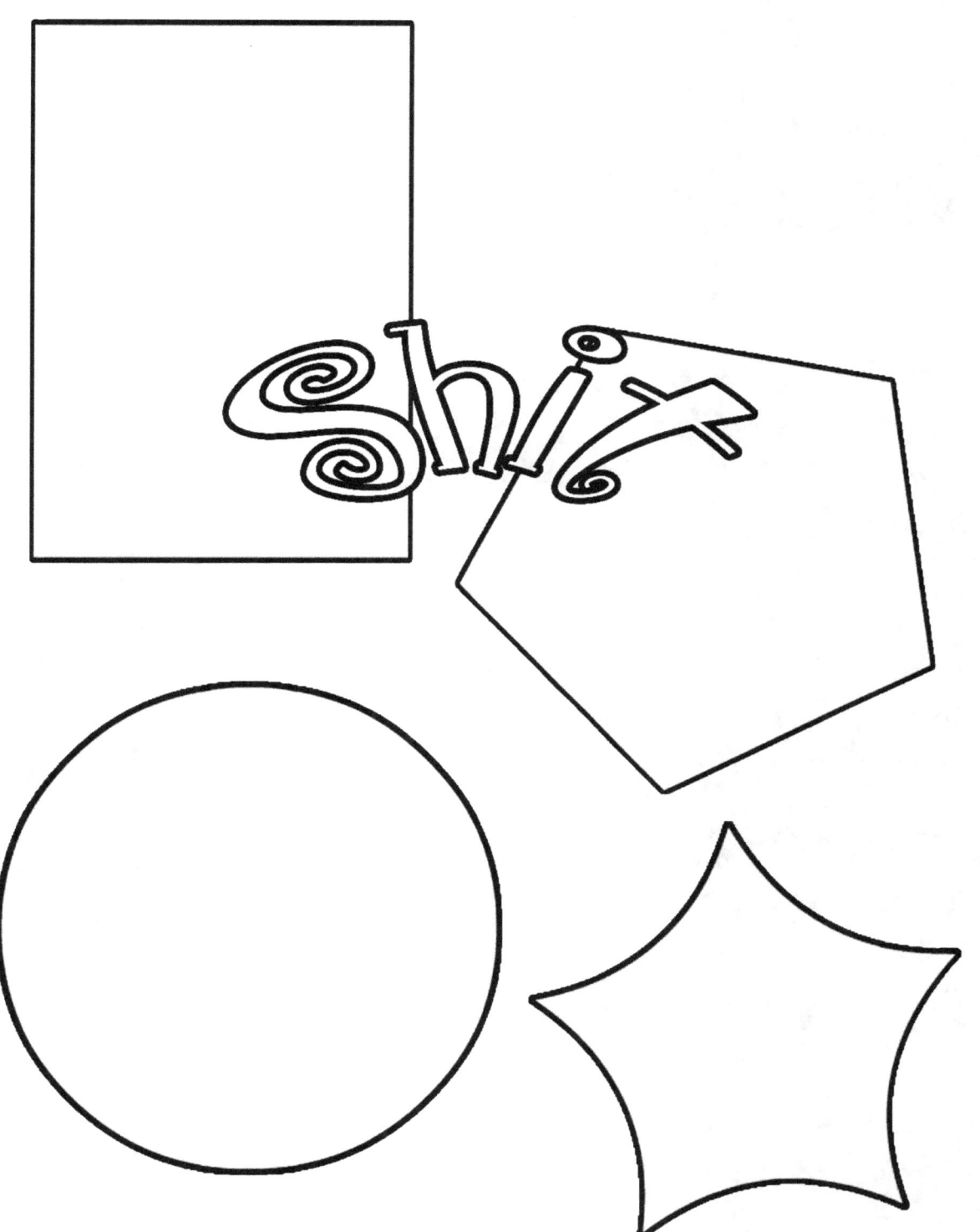

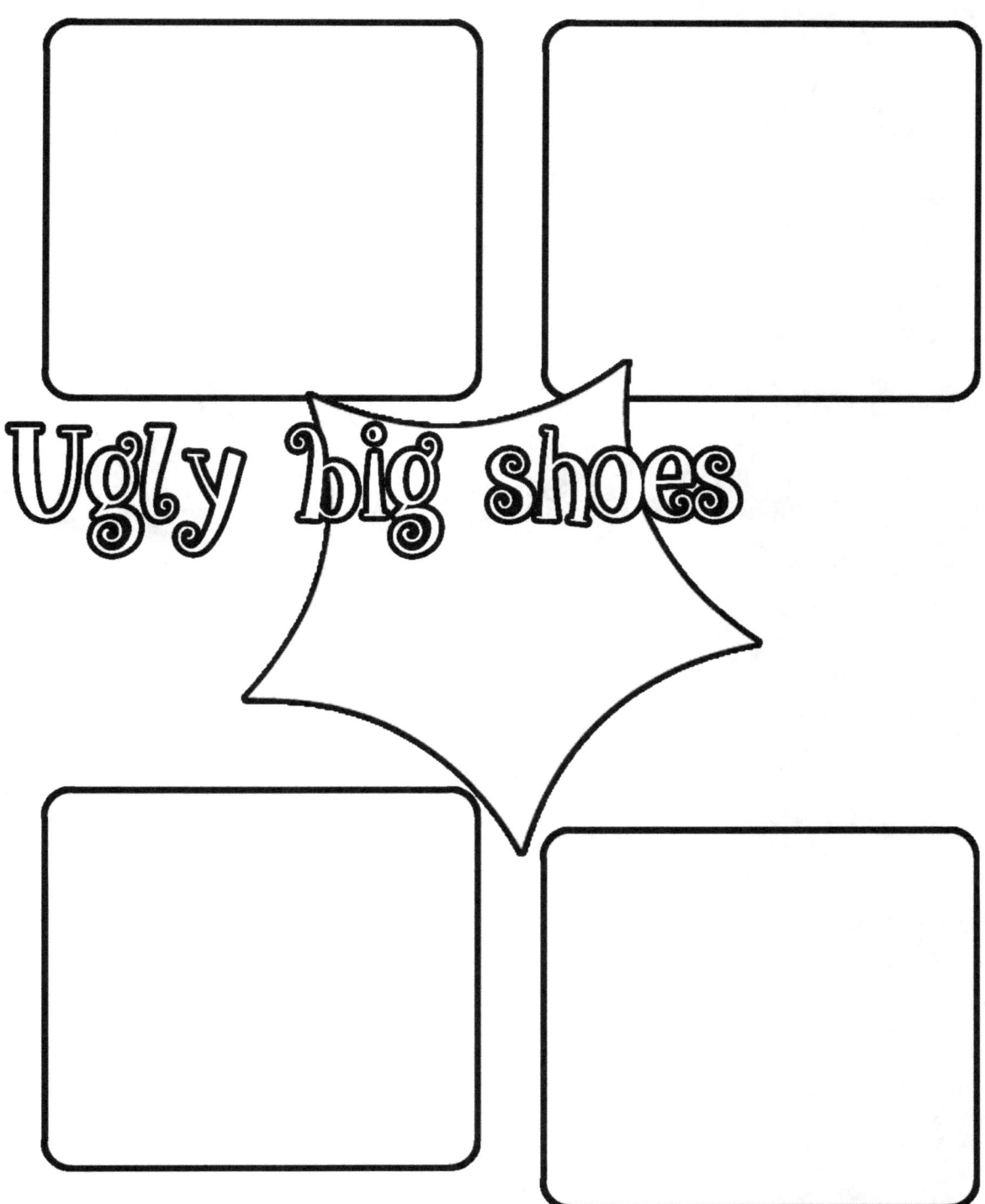

Ugly big shoes

Douche bag

Dick Midget

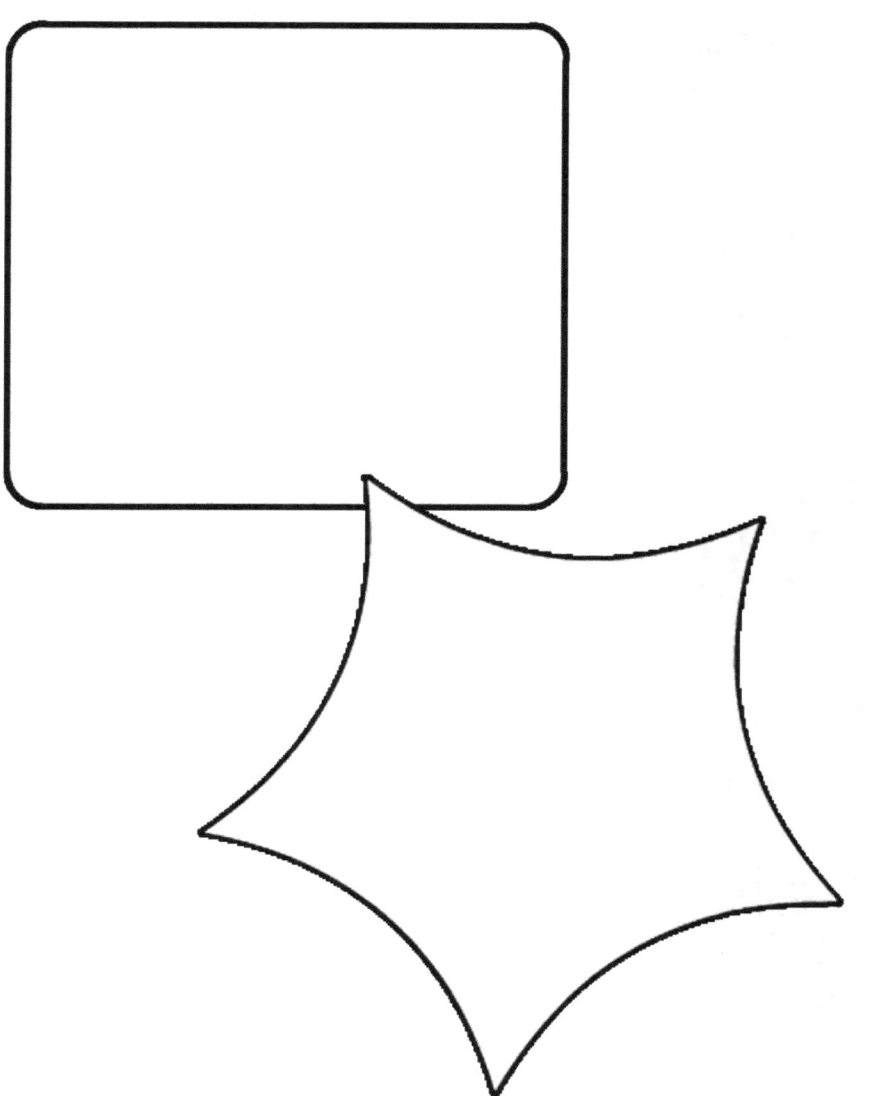

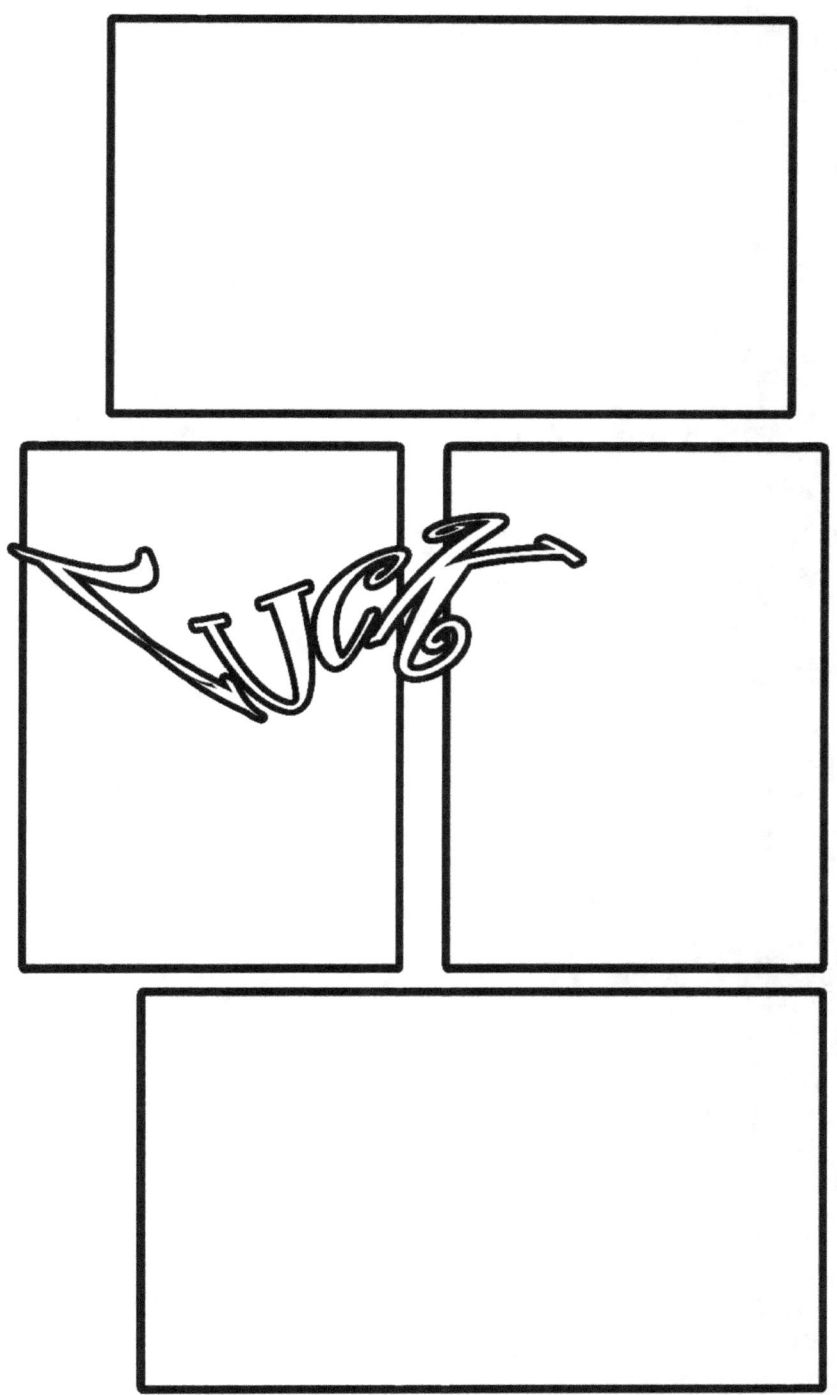

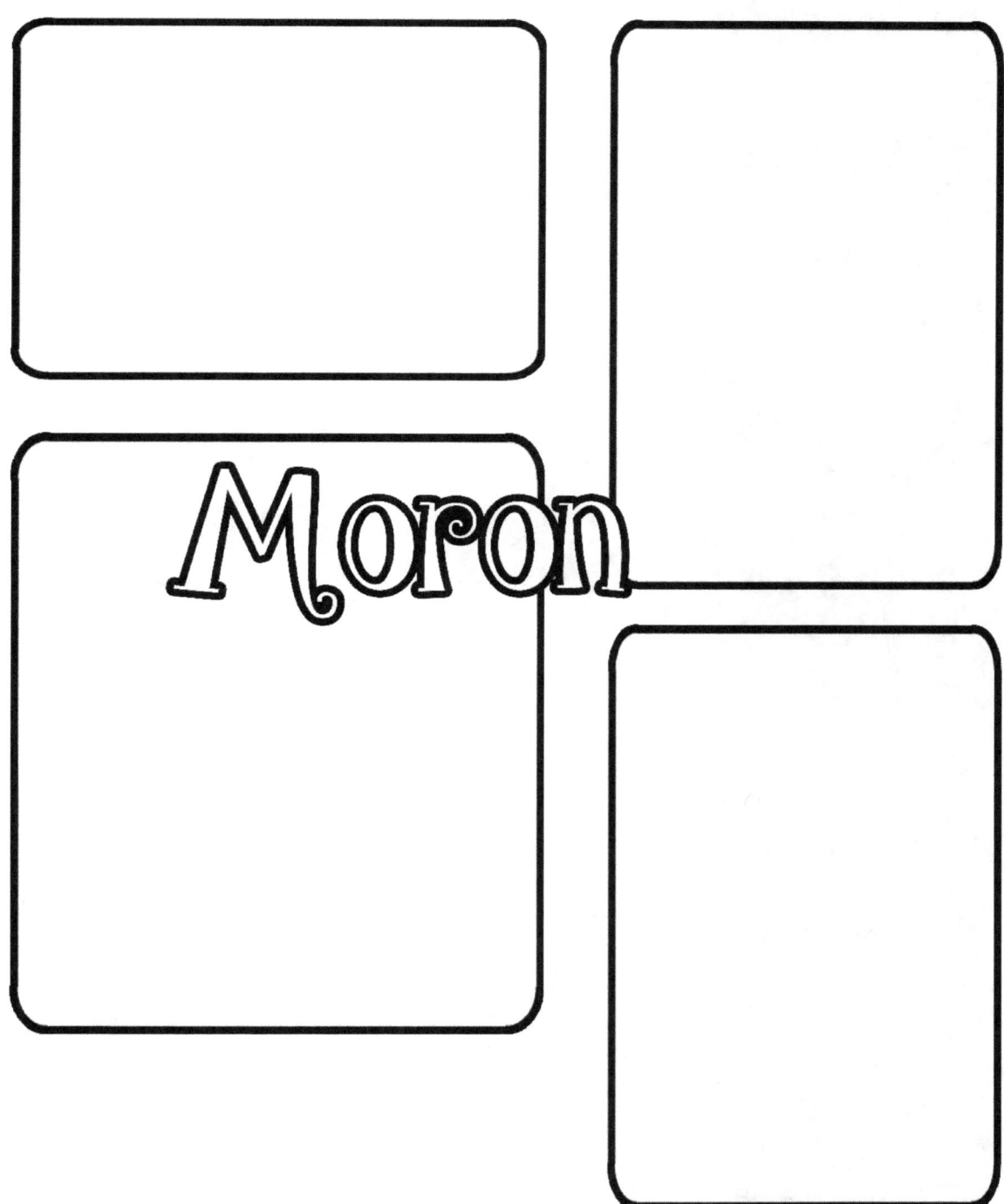

Moron

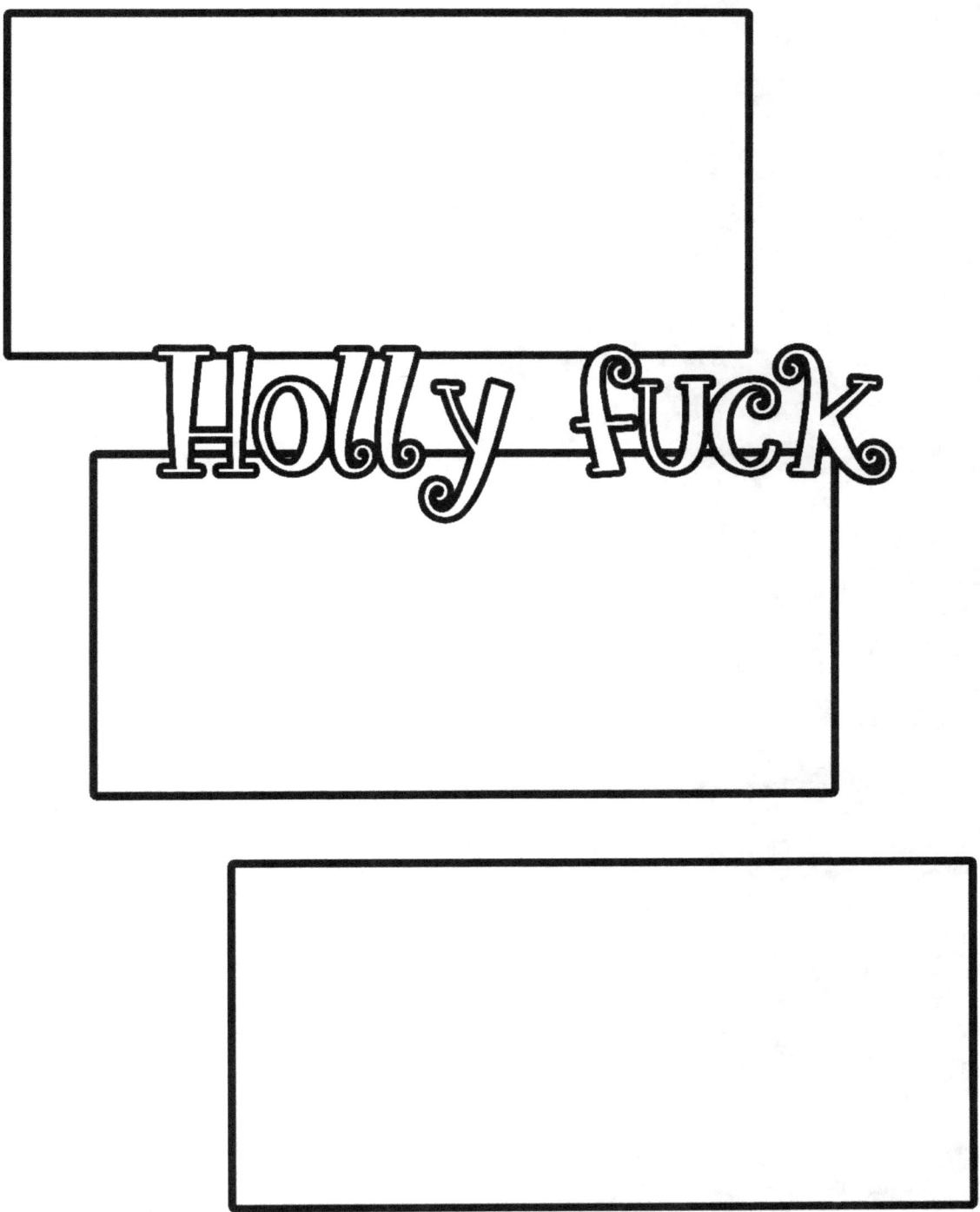

Holly fuck

Dipshitidiot

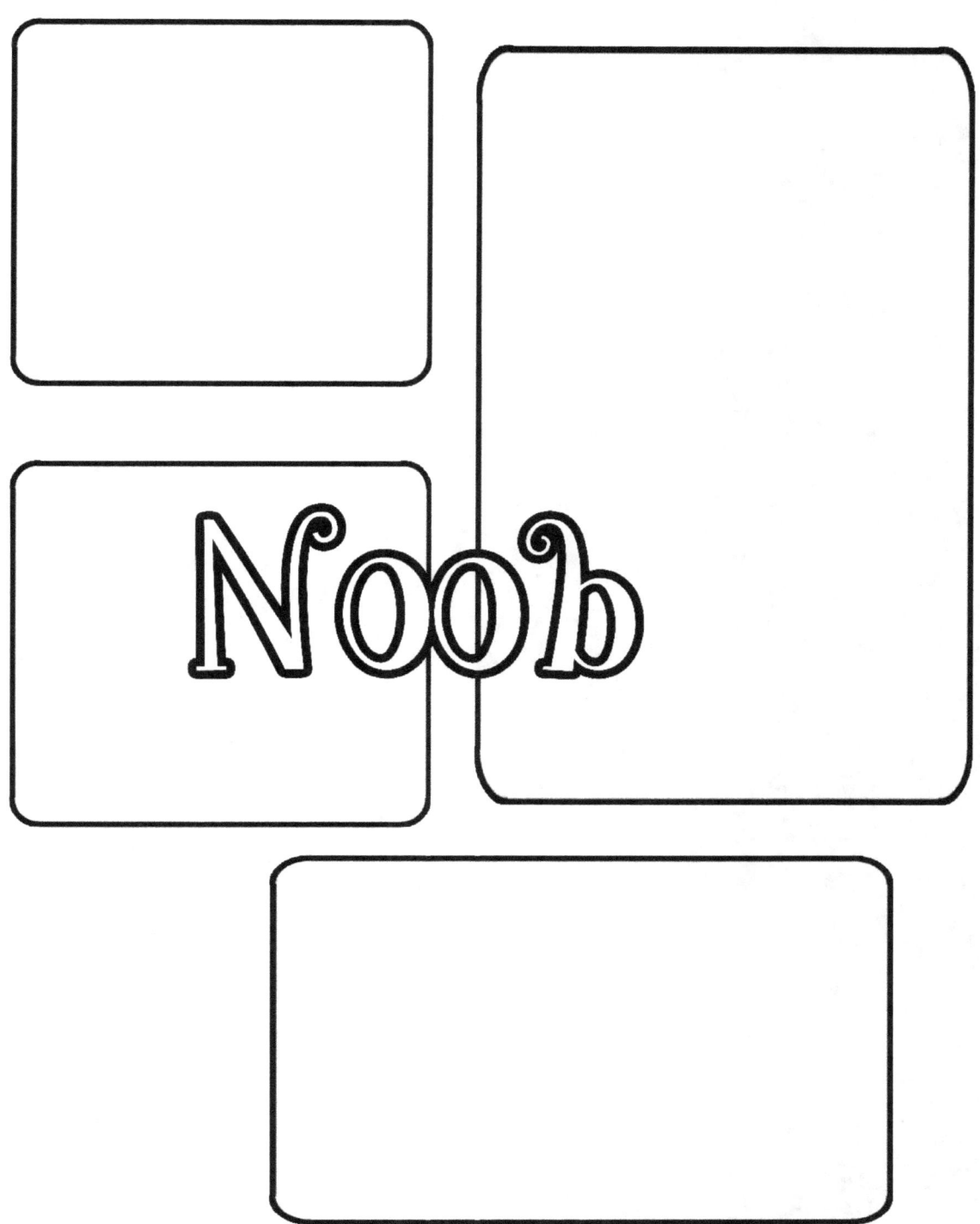

www.ingramcontent.com/pod-product-compliance
Lightning Source LLC
Chambersburg PA
CBHW081125180526
45170CB00008B/3012